EDGE BOOKS™

# U.S. MARINES by the Numbers

by Elizabeth Raum

Consultant: Raymond L. Puffer, PhD
Historian, Retired
Edwards Air Force Base History Office

CAPSTONE PRESS
a capstone imprint

Edge Books are published by Capstone Press,
1710 Roe Crest Drive, North Mankato, Minnesota 56003
www.capstonepub.com

**Library of Congress Cataloging-in-Publication Data**
Raum, Elizabeth.
  U.S. Marines by the numbers / by Elizabeth Raum.
      pages cm. — (Edge. Military by the numbers)
  Includes bibliographical references and index.
  Summary: "Describes aspects of the U.S. Marines using numbers, stats, and
infographics"— Provided by publisher.
  Audience: Grades 4 to 6.
  ISBN 978-1-4765-3919-5 (library binding)
  ISBN 978-1-4765-5122-7 (paperback)
  ISBN 978-1-4765-5967-4 (eBook PDF)
1. United States. Marine Corps—Juvenile literature. I. Title.
  VE23.R42 2014
  359.9'60973—dc23                                                  2013032522

* Numbers based on 2013 information unless otherwise noted

**Editorial Credits**
Mandy Robbins and Brenda Haugen, editors; Heidi Thompson, designer;
Danielle Ceminsky, production specialist

**Photo Credits**
AP Images: Joe Rosenthal, 12-13; Corbis: Bettmann, 10 (bottom), 11 (bottom), Peter
Turnley, 29 (bottom left); Getty Images: Bert Hardy, 11 (top), Buyenlarge, 10 (inset); Naval
History & Heritage Command/U.S. Navy map, 13 (inset); PEOSoldier, 20 (bottom);
Shutterstock: arimdambanerjee, 26, Konstantnin, 20 (top), Vartanov Anatoly, 21 (middle);
U.S. Marine Corps photo by Cpl. Benjamin R. Reynolds, 22 (top), Cpl. Dwight A.
Henderson, 8-9, Cpl. Eric Quintanillla, 14 (top right), Cpl. Liz Gleason, 19 (top left), Cpl.
Mace M. Gratz, cover, Cpl. Marionne T. Mangrum, 29 (bottom), Cpl. Michael Augusto,
23 (bottom), Cpl. Michael S. Cifuentes, 23 (top), Cpl. Richard Blumenstein, 28-29, Cpl.
Walter D. Marino II, 14 (top left), 19 (top right), Gunnery Sgt. Kevin W. Williams, 22
(bottom), Gunnery Sgt. Scott Dunn, 22 (middle), Lance Cpl. Bridget M. Keane, 19 (bottom
both), Lance Cpl. Codey Underwood, 16-17, Lance Cpl. Crystal Druery, 14 (bottom
right), Lance Cpl. Jacob W. Chase, 21 (top), Lance Cpl. Jhonson Simeon, 27 (top), Lance
Cpl. Kyle McNally, 29 (top right), Lance Cpl. Matthew Manning, 27 (bottom), Lance Cpl.
Michael Ito, 14 (bottom left), Lance Cpl. Pedro Cardenas, 18 (bottom), Lance Cpl. Scott
W. Whiting, 6 (bottom), Pfc. Crystal Druery, 18 (top), Pfc. Dalton Precht, 21 (bottom),
Pfc. Kasey Peacock, 20 (middle), Sgt. Jose Nava, 14 (background), Staff Sgt. Danielle M.
Bacon, 29 (top), U.S. Navy photo by MC3 Jonathan Sunderman, back cover, 24-25, MCSA
Daniel J. Walls, 4, Seaman Trevor Welsh, 6 (top)

**Design Elements**
Shutterstock: Akai37, Darq, Filip Bjorkman, kednert, MIRJANA BANJAC, Paul Stringer,
URRRA, Yaraz, zsooofija

Printed in the United States of America in Stevens Point, Wisconsin.
092013      007768WZS14

# Table of Contents

# First to Fight

Who does the United States government call in an emergency? The Marines! The United States Marine Corps, a branch of the United States Navy, is a rapid-reaction force. Check out the numbers that back up the U.S. Marines.

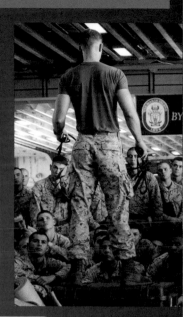

In conflicts, a Marine Expeditionary Unit (MEU) is often the first force on the ground. An MEU can be called to action at any moment. An MEU includes 2,200 ground and air combat troops, their commanders, and the logistics crews that provide communications, vehicles, and supplies.

An MEU can go from first alert to action in just 6 hours.

**hour 1** Marine commanders receive orders.

**hour 2** Marine commanders and staff develop an action plan.

**hour 3** Marine ground, aviation, and logistics crews get ready to help with the mission.

**hour 4** Commander approves the plan and sends out orders for each Marine.

**hour 5** Marines prepare to move out, loading their gear onto vehicles.

**hour 6** The first wave of Marines is sent in.

"**Marines.** The Few, the Proud."

| | All Armed Services | Marines | Percentage of total that are Marines |
|---|---|---|---|
| Total Military Personnel | 1,431,000 | 202,441 | 14% |
| Officers | 234,000 | 21,307 | 9% |
| Enlisted | 1,183,200 | 181,134 | 15% |

4

*based on 2010 information

# Officers

**Male 93.8%** 20,498
**Female 6.2%** 1,348

1 👮 = 1,000 officers

# Enlisted

**Male 92.9%** 166,983
**Female 7.1%** 12,352

1 🪖 = 1,000 soldiers

logistics——activities that support fighting units, including transport, supply, communications, and medical aid
aviation——having to do with building and flying aircraft
enlisted——the people in the armed forces who are not officers

# Marines by 7s

## MEUs

7

ready to respond to
a crisis at any time.

## 7 days

| Sun. | Mon. | Tue. | Wed. | Thur. | Fri. | Sat. |
|------|------|------|------|-------|------|------|
|      |      |      |      |       |      |      |

a Marine's workweek

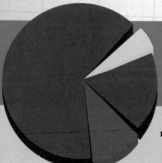

**7.6%**
enlisted Marines ages 31-35

**17.5%**
enlisted Marines ages 26-30

# 7,331

Spouses of Marines who
are also in the military

## 7.9 lb.

weight of M27 Marine
Infantry Automatic Rifle

**17** age of youngest enlisted Marines

**77** days of constant attack that Marines endured in 1968 while defending the American base at Khe Sanh during the Vietnam War (1959–1975)

**70%** percentage of Marines serving first enlistment

**1775** year the Marines were founded

**17,500** miles per hour speed that Marine Corps Colonel John Glenn traveled when he became the first American to orbit Earth in 1962

spouse—husband or wife
enlistment—time of military service

# Careers in the Marines

**Infantry:** fighting force

**32,749** Infantry Marines (all men)*

**42** major job categories

**293** specific roles

*In 2013 the Pentagon lifted its ban on women in combat roles.

Machine gunners
**10%**

Reconnaissance men
**2%**

Antitank Missilemen
**7%**

Infantry Assaultmen
**6%**

**60%**
Infantrymen

**15%**
Mortarmen

# Aviation Ordnance: Provide, maintain, and transport ordnance

**2,831** Marines

**2,651** Men

**180** Women

# Motor Transport:

Mechanics and vehicle operators

**14,762** Marines
**14,087** Men
**675** Women

QUANTITY

| 12 | 3 | 100 | 57 | 13 |
|---|---|---|---|---|
| M998 | M936 | M923 | M105A2 | M149A1 |

# Military Police: Military Police & Corrections

**4,977** Marines

**4,619** Men

**358** Women

reconnaissance—a mission to gather information about an enemy
ordnance—military weapons, ammunition, and maintenance equipment

# Marine Corps in the 20th Century

## U.S. Involvement in World War I (1914–1918)

**2** years of major U.S. engagements

**9,520** Marines wounded in action

**31,600** total Marines serving in war zone

**2,461** Marines killed in battle

## U.S. Involvement in World War II (1939–1945)

**4** years, 8 months of major U.S. engagements

**67,207** Marines wounded in action

**485,883** Marines serving in war zone

**19,733** Marines killed in battle

# U.S. Involvement in the Korean War (1950—1953)

**4** years of major U.S. engagements

about **130,000** total Marines serving in war zone

**23,744** Marines wounded in action

**4,268** Marines killed in battle

# U.S. Involvement in the Vietnam War

(1959—1975)

Vietnam was the longest and bloodiest war in Marine history.

**13,095** Marines killed in battle

**88,594** Marines wounded in action

**794,000** total Marines serving in war zone

**7** years of major U.S. engagements

11

# Iwo Jima

## A Great Marine Victory

### The Battle of Iwo Jima

**Dates:** February 19 to March 26, 1945

**What:** defining World War II battle

**Where:** Pacific Ocean south of Japan

**Goal:** capture island of Iwo Jima from Japanese Empire

**Result:** Japan surrendered the island to the Marines

**3** number of Marines pictured in Rosenthal's photo who died in the battle after the flag-raising

**2** number of U.S. flags Marines raised atop Mt. Suribachi

1st flag raised: 10:30 a.m.

2nd flag raised: 12 p.m.

The second flag was larger than the first and is the event famously captured by photographer Joe Rosenthal.

About **22,000** Japanese troops dug **11** miles of underground tunnels.

**36** days of battle

**700** ships transported Marines and cargo to Iwo Jima.

**77,000** Marines from 3rd, 4th, and 5th Marine divisions took part in the battle.

Of the **22,000** Japanese soldiers, only about **1,100** survived.

More than **21,000** Marines were wounded.
Nearly **7,000** Marines died.

**1/3** of all Marines killed in World War II died on Iwo Jima.

**27** Medals of Honor were awarded, **13** posthumously.

# Iwo Jima:

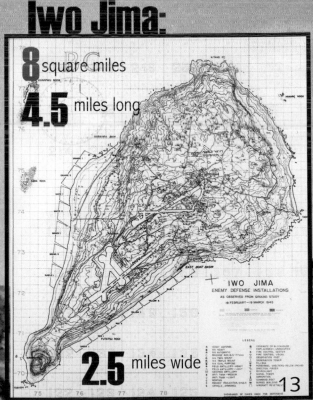

**8** square miles

**4.5** miles long

**2.5** miles wide

posthumous—coming or happening after death

13

# Becoming a Marine

## Basic Training

The physical requirements of basic training are different for men and women. In all other training, men and women must meet the same standards.

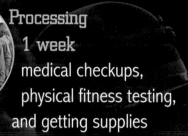

Processing
1 week
medical checkups,
physical fitness testing,
and getting supplies

Phase 1
4 weeks
physical conditioning;
self-defense; marching;
Marine Corps customs,
history, and values training;
weapons training, first aid training

Phase 2
4 weeks
water survival and
weapons marksmanship

Phase 3
4 weeks
basic warrior skills;
defensive driving
course; land navigation;
basic field skills

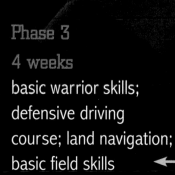

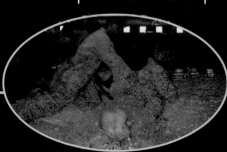

# Activity

## Hours Spent
in Basic Training

187: Eating

13: Marching

572: Sleeping

34.5: Drill practice

41: Academic studies

34: Ethics and values training

54: The Crucible (final testing)

5: On-base liberty on Family Day

60: Senior drill instructor time

106: Free time (includes 4-5 hours on Sundays & holidays)

146: Daily routine (showering, grooming, caring for clothing and room)

81: Physical training/conditioning

225.5: Instruction time (combat, water survival, weapons, field training)

# Contents of a Marine Recruit's Seabag

**1**

- reflective safety belt
- desert cap
- woodland cap
- field desert
  boonie cap
- green sweatshirt
- pair green
  sweatpants
- pair combat boots
- pair jungle boots

- pair shower shoes
- pair running shoes
- pair book bands
- hygiene kit
- sewing kit
- green towel
- green washcloth
- flashlight
- jock strap
- mouthpiece

- boot brush
- pair of gloves
- poncho
- cartridge belt
- canteen cup
- Gore-Tex® top
- pillow
- plastic pillowcase
- fabric pillowcase
- mattress cover

**2**
- duffel bags
- khaki belts with gold-plated tips
- pairs of woodland trousers
- woodland blouses
- laundry bags
- 1-quart canteens
- canteen covers
- blankets
- sheets

**3**
- gym trunks
- pairs of desert trousers
- desert blouses
- pairs of white socks

**6**
- undershirts
- pairs of brown boot socks
- pairs of underwear

# The Crucible:
## A Rite of Passage

All Marines go through 12 weeks of intense training during boot camp. That training leads up to a final combat exercise called The Crucible.

**29:** number of problem-solving exercises performed

**54:** number of hours The Crucible lasts

**48:** number of miles marched

**45:** pounds of gear carried

**24:** number of logs climbed over and under while carrying supplies

# 36
## stations

including exercises such as:

crossing two horizontal
cable-supported logs

working as a team to overcome
obstacles in an exercise called 12 Stalls

climbing 8-foot-high
horizontal log

crossing 52-foot-long
ropes carrying
ammunition cans and
water cans

climbing up and down a 10-foot
wall on a knotted rope

retrieving "wounded" dummy
from top of 18-foot tower

carrying supplies across two 52-foot-long
ropes suspended 2 feet and 10 feet off
the ground

# Equipping the Marines

Weapons

## M16
service rifle
Ammunition: 5.56 x 45 mm rounds
Maximum Range: 3,600 meters
Rate of Fire: 12 to 15 rounds a minute

## M203
grenade launcher
Ammunition: 40 mm grenades
Maximum Range: 350 meters
Rate of Fire: single-shot

## M249 SAW
automatic weapon
Ammunition: 5.56 x 45 mm rounds
Maximum Range: 3,600 meters
Rate of Fire: 85 rounds a minute

# M777 Howitzer

long-range cannon
Ammunition: 155 mm / 39-caliber rounds
Maximum Range: 30 kilometers
Rate of Fire: 5 rounds a minute

## M9 Beretta

lightweight pistol
Ammunition: 9 mm rounds
Maximum Range: 50 meters
Rate of Fire: semiautomatic

## FGM-148 Javelin

missile
Ammunition: missiles
Maximum Range: 2,500 meters
Rate of Fire: single-shot

# Distance

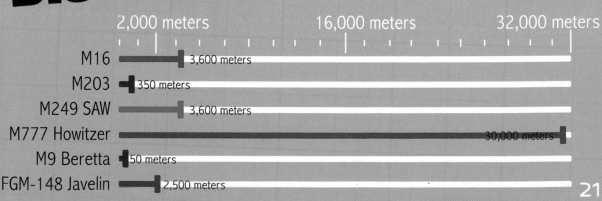

| | 2,000 meters | 16,000 meters | 32,000 meters |
|---|---|---|---|
| M16 | 3,600 meters | | |
| M203 | 350 meters | | |
| M249 SAW | 3,600 meters | | |
| M777 Howitzer | | | 30,000 meters |
| M9 Beretta | 50 meters | | |
| FGM-148 Javelin | 2,500 meters | | |

# M-ATV

What: all-terrain vehicle
Weight: 25,000 lb.
Size: 20.5 ft. long; 8.2 ft. wide

## AAV-7

What: **amphibious** assault vehicle
Weight: 26 tons (fully loaded with a three-man crew)
Capacity: 21 combat-loaded Marines, 3 crew members, 10,000 lb. of cargo

## LAV

What: armored fighting tank
Weight: 24,980 lb.
Crew: 3-man crew
Weapons: 2 grenade launchers, 25 mm cannon, two M240 machine guns

# Vehicles

amphibious—a vehicle or craft that can travel over land and also over or in water

## HMMWV

What: high mobility multipurpose
wheeled vehicle
Weight: 5,200 lb.
Special features: armored plating,
bullet-resistant glass

## MTVR

What: crew and supply transport vehicle
Weight: 7 tons
Capacity: 20 tons

Top Speeds

AAV-7

45 mph

LAV

62.5 mph

M-ATV

HMMWV

# The MV-22B Osprey

The MV-22B Osprey was first used in combat in 2007. It increased the Marines' ability to outmaneuver their enemies. The Osprey has the speed and range of an airplane, but it takes off and lands like a helicopter. It can carry 24 combat Marines from a ship to a land base. The Osprey can go twice as fast and five times farther than previous helicopters.

Weight

**52,600** lb.

Cost per unit

**$72-$95** million

Wingspan
**84.6** ft.

Range
**990** miles

Crew
**3** [ pilot
   [ copilot
   [ crew chief

Cruising Speed
**322** miles per hour

Capacity
**24** combat troops

Length
**57** ft., **3** in.

Height
**22** ft., **1** in.

# Beyond the Battlefield

## Marine Corps Disaster Relief

The Marine Corps seeks to make the world a safer, better place. Part of that mission involves providing emergency relief when natural disasters hit.

## Earthquake in Haiti (January 2010)

The 24th Marine Expeditionary Unit delivered and distributed:

**57,368 meals**

**1,365,617** lb. of rice

**589,764** bottles of water

**2,781** hand-crank radios

**22,064** lb. of medical supplies

**79,656** jars of baby food

more than **1,000,000** disaster relief rations

 **15,207** lb. of other supplies

# Flooding in Pakistan

(August 2010)

**2,200**
Marines responded.

U.S. helicopters rescued **3,075** people.

Marines delivered
**650,000**
lb. of relief supplies.

# Typhoon in the Philippines

(December 2010)

**500** relief aid boxes

**165 tons**
of relief supplies
delivered, including:

**40** generators

**250** boxes of blankets

**14,500** family ration packs

**49,000** lb. of rice

**833** sleeping mats

**147** bundles of mosquito nets

ration——a family's daily share of food
generator——a machine that produces electricity by turning
a magnet inside a coil of wire

27

# Marine Special Operations

Marine Special Operations units are small teams trained to work with foreign armies, defeat terrorists, gather sensitive information, and complete other missions.

Marine Special Operations Command (MARSOC) was activated in 2006. The Marine Special Operations Regiments (MSOR) are combat units based on those used in a 2003 pilot program. In that program, a unit was composed of:

## 30-man reconnaissance team

## 29-man intelligence team

## 7-man combat team

## 1 headquarters team

Today 2,500 Marines are in Special Operations. Each highly trained unit is sent overseas as needed.

# Marine Special Operations Training

**Phase 1**    10 weeks    swimming, running, rucking, hand-to-hand combat, mission planning, fire support, land navigation, combat medic training

**Phase 2**    8 weeks

intelligence gathering, sea navigation, small boat handling, field training in urban and non-urban environments

5 weeks    **Phase 3**

close-quarters combat, marksmanship, shooting and moving as a team

7 weeks    **Phase 4**

how to think like the enemy in order to stop acts of terror, guerilla warfare, or rebellion

intelligence—secret information about an enemy's plans or actions
ruck—to hike carrying heavy weight in a backpack; ruck is a military term for "backpack"
urban—having to do with a city
guerilla warfare—a type of military action using small groups of fighters to carry out surprise attacks against enemy forces

# Glossary

**amphibious** (am-FI-bee-uhs)—a vehicle or craft that can travel over land and also over or in water

**aviation** (ay-vee-AY-shuhn)—having to do with building and flying aircraft

**enlisted** (en-LIS-tuhd)—the people in the armed forces who are not officers

**enlistment** (en-LIST-muhnt)—time of military service

**generator** (JEN-uh-ray-tur)—a machine that produces electricity by turning a magnet inside a coil of wire

**guerilla warfare** (gur-RIL-lah WOR-fair)—a type of military action using small groups of fighters to carry out surprise attacks against enemy forces

**intelligence** (in-TEL-uh-jenss)—secret information about an enemy's plans or actions

**logistics** (luh-JIS-ticks)—activities that support fighting units, including transport, supply, communications, and medical aid

**ordnance** (ORD-nuhnss)—military weapons, ammunition, and maintenance equipment

**posthumous** (POHST-chuh-muhss)—coming or happening after death

**ration** (RASH-uhn)—a family's daily share of food

**reconnaissance** (ree-KAH-nuh-suhnss)—a mission to gather information about an enemy

**ruck** (RUCK)—to hike carrying heavy weight in a ruck or backpack

**spouse** (SPOUSS)—husband or wife

**urban** (UR-buhn)—having to do with a city

# Read More

**Sandler, Michael.** *Marine Force Recon in Action.* Special Ops. New York: Bearport Pub., 2008.

**Schwartz, Heather E.** *Women of the U.S. Marine Corps: Breaking Barriers.* Women in the Armed Forces. Mankato, Minn.: Capstone Press, 2011.

**Sodaro, Craig.** *The U.S. Marines Special Operations Regiment: The Missions.* American Special Ops. North Mankato, Minn.: Capstone Press, 2013.

# Internet Sites

FactHound offers a safe, fun way to find Internet sites related to this book. All of the sites on FactHound have been researched by our staff.

Here's all you do:

Visit *www.facthound.com*

Type in this code: 9781476539195

 Check out projects, games and lots more at **www.capstonekids.com**

# Index

## Titles in this set:

**U.S. AIR FORCE** by the **Numbers**

**U.S. MARINES** by the **Numbers**

**U.S. ARMY** by the **Numbers**

**U.S. NAVY** by the **Numbers**